CAKES
&
BAKES

CAKES & BAKES

A MOUTH-WATERING
COLLECTION OF OVER
50 RECIPES FOR DREAMY
CAKES AND BAKES

This edition published in 2012
LOVE FOOD is an imprint of Parragon Books Ltd

Parragon
Chartist House
15–17 Trim Street
Bath, BA1 1HA, UK

ISBN: 978-1-4075-7439-4

Printed in China

Designed by Fiona Roberts
Cover by Talking Design
Recipes and photography by The Bridgewater Book Company Ltd.

Notes for the Reader
This book uses both metric and imperial measurements. Follow the same units of measurement throughout; do not mix metric and imperial. All spoon measurements are level: teaspoons are assumed to be 5 ml, and tablespoons are assumed to be 15 ml. Unless otherwise stated, milk is assumed to be full fat, eggs and individual vegetables are medium, and pepper is freshly ground black pepper.

Garnishes, decorations and serving suggestions are all optional and not necessarily included in the recipe ingredients or method.

The times given are an approximate guide only. Preparation times differ according to the techniques used by different people and the cooking times may also vary from those given. Optional ingredients, variations or serving suggestions have not been included in the time calculations.

Recipes using raw or very lightly cooked eggs should be avoided by infants, the elderly, pregnant women, convalescents and anyone suffering from an illness. Pregnant and breastfeeding women are advised to avoid eating peanuts and peanut products. Sufferers from nut allergies should be aware that some of the ready-made ingredients used in the recipes in this book may contain nuts. Always check the packaging before use.

CONTENTS

Time for some home-baking...

There is something special about home-baked cakes. It's not just that they are really delicious, nor even that they are delightfully different from those you can buy in the supermarket. It's more that they always seem like a delectable treat – and this is as true of a batch of easy-to-make muffins as it is of a richly decorated chocolate gateau. Home-made cakes and slices turn any occasion into a special one, whether served at a fund-raising coffee morning, an old-fashioned afternoon tea party or as a luxurious dessert at the end of a celebratory meal. They also make great after-school snacks and any-time-of-day nibbles when you need a pick-me-up.

There are several basic techniques, all of which are easy to master. These include creaming, rubbing-in, melting and whisking and individual recipes provide clear instructions in the method. However, there are a few tips that are worth noting.

creaming: Fat and sugar are creamed together, that is beaten with a wooden spoon or an electric mixer, until the mixture is light and fluffy and has incorporated plenty of air. Butter produces a richer flavour than margarine, although either can be used. Unsalted butter is best for cakes and other sweet baking. Caster sugar is usually used as it is finer than granulated, but the type will always be specified in the recipe. When the fat and sugar are completely combined and aerated, the eggs are added. To avoid curdling, that is the mixture separating, eggs should always be beaten in gradually. If the mixture does begin to curdle, beat in a tablespoonful of flour before adding any more egg. Finally, the dry ingredients, such as flour, baking powder and cocoa powder, are folded in. Use a metal spoon or rubber spatula and gently stir in the flour using a figure-of-eight movement in order to avoid knocking out the air. Add the dry ingredients gradually and always sift them first.

rubbing-in: Fat is incorporated into the dry ingredients by rubbing it in with the fingertips or working it in with a pastry blender. The flour and other fine ingredients should be sifted into the bowl first and the fat – butter or margarine – is added. Cut it into the flour so that it is in small pieces, then rub in with the fingertips only, lifting the mixture high up in the bowl to incorporate air. Sugar may be stirred into the mixture before the fat is rubbed in but it is more usual to add it afterwards, just before incorporating the liquid – commonly eggs or milk. Knead lightly to make sure that everything is thoroughly incorporated but try to avoid handling the mixture too much.

melting: Melted fat is beaten into sifted dry ingredients until the mixture is fully combined. This is a particularly easy method. Sift the dry ingredients into a bowl and set aside. Cut the fat – usually butter or margarine – into pieces and gently heat it in a small saucepan with any other specified ingredients, such as syrup, treacle or, sometimes, sugar, until melted and blended. Be careful not to overheat. Then either beat in the dry ingredients or beat the melted mixture into the dry ingredients according to the recipe.

whisking: In this method it is the eggs that are whisked. These may be whole or separated – the recipe will specify. Once plenty of air has been incorporated, dry ingredients, such as flour, cornflour and baking powder, should be gently folded in (see creaming opposite). There is no additional fat and cakes made by this method are very light.

top tips

✳ Don't substitute low-fat spreads for butter or margarine as their high water content makes them unsuitable for baking.

✳ Never measure liquid flavourings, such as almond essence, directly over the mixing bowl as it is easy to pour too much into the spoon which then splashes into the cake mixture. Take similar care when adding food colouring.

✳ Always use the size and shape of cake tin specified in the recipe and grease and/or line it as described. Unsalted butter is best for greasing as it is less likely to burn.

✳ Always preheat the oven to the required temperature and resist the temptation to open the oven door frequently. When checking the cake, open the oven door gently and only slightly, as a sudden draught is likely to make it 'fall'.

✳ Test a cake for 'doneness' by pressing the top lightly with your fingertip. If the cake springs back immediately, it is ready. If your finger leaves a small dent, it requires further cooking. Alternatively, insert a wooden cocktail stick into the centre of the cake. If it comes out clean, the cake is ready.

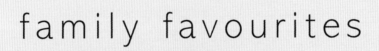

family favourites

Victoria Sandwich

easy

serves 8–10

prep: 25 minutes + cooling

25–30 minutes cooking

175 g/6 oz unsalted butter, softened, plus extra for greasing
175 g/6 oz caster sugar
3 eggs, beaten
175 g/6 oz self-raising flour
3 tbsp jam or lemon curd, and 1 tbsp caster or icing sugar, to serve

Preheat the oven to 180°C/350°F/Gas Mark 4. Grease 2 x 20-cm/8-inch sandwich tins with a little butter and line the bases with baking parchment.

Put the butter and sugar in a mixing bowl and cream together until the mixture is pale and light and fluffy. Cream for 1–2 minutes if using an electric whisk, or 5–6 minutes by hand. Add the eggs, a little at a time, beating well after each addition.

Sift the flour and carefully add it to the mixture, folding it in with a metal spoon or a palette knife.

Divide the mixture between the prepared sandwich tins and smooth over with the palette knife. Bake on the same shelf in the centre of the preheated oven for 25–30 minutes until well risen, golden brown and beginning to shrink from the sides of the tins. Remove from the oven and let them stand for 1 minute. Use a palette knife to loosen the cakes from the edge of the tins.

Turn the cakes out onto a clean tea towel and remove the lining paper. Invert the cakes onto a cooling tray (this prevents the cooling tray from marking the top of the cakes). Leave for 30–45 minutes in a cool place to cool completely. Sandwich together with jam or lemon curd, and sprinkle over the sugar.

Carrot Cake

Preheat the oven to 190°C/375°F/Gas Mark 5. Grease a 23-cm/9-inch square cake tin with a little butter and line with baking parchment. In a mixing bowl, beat the eggs until well blended and add the sugar and oil. Mix well. Add the grated carrot.

Sift in the flour, bicarbonate of soda and spices, then add the walnuts. Mix everything together until well incorporated.

Spread the mixture into the prepared cake tin and bake in the centre of the preheated oven for 40–50 minutes until the cake is nicely risen, firm to the touch and has begun to shrink away slightly from the edge of the tin.

Remove from the oven and leave to cool in the tin until just warm, then turn out onto a cooling rack.

To make the topping, put all the ingredients into a mixing bowl and beat together for 2–3 minutes until really smooth.

When the cake is completely cold, spread with the topping, smooth over with a fork and leave to firm up a little before cutting into 16 portions. Store in an airtight tin in a cool place for up to 1 week.

easy

makes 16 pieces

prep: 30 minutes

40–50 minutes cooking

butter, for greasing
2 eggs
175 g/6 oz muscovado sugar
200 ml/7 fl oz sunflower oil
200 g/7 oz carrot, coarsely grated
225 g/8 oz wholemeal flour
1 tsp bicarbonate of soda
2 tsp ground cinnamon
1 tsp freshly grated nutmeg
115 g/4 oz walnuts, roughly chopped

TOPPING

115 g/4 oz half-fat cream cheese
4 tbsp butter, softened
85 g/3 oz icing sugar
1 tsp grated lemon rind
1 tsp grated orange rind

Caraway Madeira

easy

serves 8

prep: 25 minutes + cooling

1 hour cooking

225 g/8 oz butter, softened, plus extra for greasing
175 g/6 oz soft brown sugar
3 eggs, beaten
350 g/12 oz self-raising flour
1 tbsp caraway seeds
grated rind of 1 lemon
6 tbsp milk
1 or 2 strips of citron peel

Preheat the oven to 160°C/325°F/Gas Mark 3. Grease a 900-g/2-lb loaf tin with butter and line with baking parchment.

Cream the butter and brown sugar together in a bowl until the mixture is pale and fluffy. Gradually add the beaten eggs to the creamed mixture, beating thoroughly after each addition. Sift the flour into the bowl and gently fold into the creamed mixture in a figure-of-eight movement.

Add the caraway seeds, lemon rind and the milk and fold in until thoroughly blended. Spoon the mixture into the prepared tin and level the surface. Bake in the preheated oven for 20 minutes.

Remove the cake from the oven, place the strips of citron peel on top and return to the oven for a further 40 minutes, or until the cake is well risen and a fine metal skewer inserted into the centre comes out clean.

Leave the cake to cool in the tin for 10 minutes before turning out and transferring to a wire rack to cool completely. Serve in slices when cold.

Crunchy Fruit Cake

easy

serves 8

**prep: 25 minutes +
cooling**

1 hour cooking

*100 g/3¹/₂ oz butter, softened,
plus extra for greasing*
100g/3¹/₂ oz caster sugar
2 eggs, beaten
*50 g/1³/₄ oz self-raising flour,
sifted*
1 tsp baking powder
100 g/3¹/₂ oz polenta
225 g/8 oz mixed dried fruit
25 g/1 oz pine kernels
grated rind of 1 lemon
4 tbsp lemon juice
2 tbsp milk

Preheat the oven to 180°C/350°F/Gas Mark 4. Grease an 18-cm/7-inch round cake tin with a little butter and line the base with baking parchment.

Whisk the butter and sugar together in a bowl until light and fluffy. Whisk in the beaten eggs, a little at a time, whisking thoroughly after each addition. Gently fold the flour, baking powder and polenta into the mixture until thoroughly blended. Stir in the mixed dried fruit, pine kernels, grated lemon rind, lemon juice and milk.

Spoon the mixture into the prepared tin and level the surface.

Bake in the preheated oven for about 1 hour, or until a fine metal skewer inserted into the centre of the cake comes out clean.

Leave the cake to cool in the tin before turning out.

Apple Streusel Cake

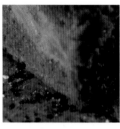

easy

serves 8

prep: 20 minutes +
40 minutes cooling

1 hour cooking

115 g/4 oz butter, plus extra for greasing
450 g/1 lb cooking apples
175 g/6 oz self-raising flour
1 tsp ground cinnamon
pinch of salt
115 g/4 oz golden caster sugar
2 eggs
1–2 tbsp milk
icing sugar, for dusting

STREUSEL TOPPING
115 g/4 oz self-raising flour
85 g/3 oz butter
85 g/3 oz golden caster sugar

Preheat the oven to 180°C/350°F/Gas Mark 4, then grease a 23-cm/9-inch round springform cake tin. To make the streusel topping, sift the flour into a bowl and rub in the butter until the mixture resembles coarse crumbs. Stir in the sugar and reserve.

Peel, core and thinly slice the apples. To make the cake, sift the flour into a bowl with the cinnamon and salt. Place the butter and sugar in a separate bowl and beat together until light and fluffy. Gradually beat in the eggs, adding a little of the flour mixture with the last addition of egg. Gently fold in half the remaining flour mixture, then fold in the rest with the milk.

Spoon the mixture into the prepared tin and smooth the top. Cover with the sliced apples and sprinkle the streusel topping evenly over the top. Bake in the preheated oven for 1 hour, or until browned and firm to the touch. Leave to cool in the tin before opening the sides. Dust the cake with icing sugar before serving.

Cherry & Almond Cake

Preheat the oven to 160°C/325°F/Gas Mark 3. Grease and line the base of an 18-cm/7-inch square cake tin. Cut the cherries in half, then place them in a sieve and rinse to remove all the syrup. Pat dry with kitchen paper and reserve.

Place the butter, caster sugar, eggs and ground almonds in a bowl. Sift in the flour and baking powder. Beat thoroughly until smooth, then stir in the cherries. Spoon the mixture into the prepared tin and smooth the top.

Sprinkle the flaked almonds over the cake. Bake in the preheated oven for 1$^{1}/_{2}$–1$^{3}/_{4}$ hours, or until well risen and a skewer inserted into the centre of the cake comes out clean. Leave to cool in the tin for 10 minutes, then turn out onto a wire rack, remove the lining paper and leave to cool.

easy

serves 8

prep: 15 minutes +
30 minutes cooling

1 hour 30 minutes–
1 hour 45 minutes
cooking

175 g/6 oz butter, softened, plus extra for greasing
225 g/8 oz glacé cherries
175 g/6 oz golden caster sugar
3 eggs
55 g/2 oz ground almonds
225 g/8 oz plain flour
1 $^{1}/_{2}$ tsp baking powder
40 g/1 $^{1}/_{2}$ oz flaked almonds

Caribbean Coconut Cake

quite easy

serves 8

**prep: 20 minutes +
30 minutes cooling**

25 minutes cooking

280 g/10 oz butter, softened,
plus extra for greasing
175 g/6 oz golden caster sugar
3 eggs
175 g/6 oz self-raising flour
1^1/$_2$ tsp baking powder
^{1}/$_2$ tsp freshly grated nutmeg
55 g/2 oz desiccated coconut
5 tbsp coconut cream
280 g/10 oz icing sugar
5 tbsp pineapple jam

TO DECORATE
toasted shredded coconut

Preheat the oven to 180°C/350°F/Gas Mark 4. Grease and line the bases of 2 x 20-cm/8-inch sandwich tins. Place 175 g/6 oz of the butter in a bowl with the sugar and eggs and sift in the flour, baking powder and nutmeg. Beat together until smooth, then stir in the coconut and 2 tablespoons of the coconut cream.

Divide the mixture between the prepared tins and smooth the tops. Bake in the preheated oven for 25 minutes, or until golden and firm to the touch. Leave to cool in the tins for 5 minutes, then turn out onto a wire rack, peel off the lining paper and leave to cool completely.

Sift the icing sugar into a bowl and add the remaining butter and coconut cream. Beat together until smooth. Spread the pineapple jam on one of the cakes and top with just under half of the buttercream. Place the other cake on top. Spread the remaining buttercream on top of the cake and scatter with toasted shredded coconut.

Pear & Ginger Cake

easy

serves 6

prep: 25 minutes +
cooling

35-40 minutes cooking

200 g/7 oz unsalted butter,
softened, plus extra for greasing
175 g/6 oz caster sugar
175 g/6 oz self-raising flour
3 tsp ground ginger
3 eggs, beaten
450 g/1 lb pears, peeled, cored
and thinly sliced, then brushed
with lemon juice
1 tbsp soft brown sugar
ice cream or double cream,
whipped lightly, to serve (optional)

Preheat the oven to 180°C/350°F/Gas Mark 4. Lightly grease a deep 20-cm/8-inch round cake tin with butter and line the base with baking parchment. Place 175 g/6 oz of the butter and the caster sugar in a bowl. Sift in the flour and ground ginger and add the eggs. Beat well with a whisk until smooth.

Spoon the cake mixture into the prepared tin and level out the surface with a palette knife. Arrange the pear slices over the cake mixture. Sprinkle with the brown sugar and dot with the remaining butter.

Bake in the preheated oven for 40 minutes, or until the cake is golden and feels springy to the touch.

Serve the pear and ginger cake warm, with ice cream or whipped cream, if you wish.

Tuscan Christmas Cake

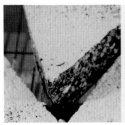

quite easy

serves 12-14

prep: 35 minutes + cooling

1 hour cooking

115 g/4 oz hazelnuts
115 g/4 oz almonds
85 g/3 oz candied peel
55 g/2 oz ready-to-eat dried apricots, chopped finely
55 g/2 oz candied pineapple, chopped finely
grated rind of 1 orange
55 g/2 oz plain flour
2 tbsp cocoa powder
1 tsp ground cinnamon
$^1/_4$ tsp ground coriander
$^1/_4$ tsp freshly grated nutmeg
$^1/_4$ tsp ground cloves
115 g/4 oz caster sugar
175 g/6 oz clear honey

TO DECORATE

icing sugar

Preheat the oven to 180°C/350°F/Gas Mark 4. Line a 20-cm/8-inch round cake tin with baking parchment. Spread out the hazelnuts on a baking sheet and toast in the preheated oven for 10 minutes, until golden brown. Tip them on to a tea towel and rub off the skins. Meanwhile, spread out the almonds on a lining paper and toast in the oven for 10 minutes, until golden. Watch carefully after 7 minutes as they can burn easily. Lower the oven temperature to 150°C/300°F/Gas Mark 2. Chop all the nuts and place in a large bowl.

Add the candied peel, apricots, pineapple and orange rind to the nuts and mix well. Sift together the flour, cocoa powder, cinnamon, coriander, nutmeg and cloves into the bowl and mix well.

Put the sugar and honey into a saucepan and set over a low heat, stirring, until the sugar has dissolved. Bring to the boil and cook for 5 minutes, until thickened and beginning to darken. Stir the nut mixture into the saucepan and remove from the heat.

Spoon the mixture into the prepared cake tin and smooth the surface with the back of a damp spoon. Bake in the preheated oven for 1 hour, then transfer to a wire rack to cool in the tin.

Carefully remove the cake from the tin and peel off the lining paper. Just before serving, dredge the top with icing sugar. Cut into thin wedges to serve.

Honey Spice Cake

Preheat the oven to 180°C/350°F/Gas Mark 4. Grease an 850-ml/
1¹/₂-pint fluted cake tin. Place the butter, sugar, honey and water into
a heavy-based saucepan. Set over a low heat and stir until the butter
has melted and the sugar has dissolved. Remove from the heat and
leave to cool for 10 minutes.

Sift the flour into a bowl and mix in the ginger, cinnamon, caraway
seeds and cardamom. Make a well in the centre. Pour in the honey
mixture and the eggs and beat well until smooth. Pour the batter into
the prepared tin and bake in the preheated oven for 40–50 minutes, or
until well risen and a skewer inserted into the centre comes out clean.
Leave to cool in the tin for 5 minutes, then transfer to a wire rack to
cool completely.

Sift the icing sugar into a bowl. Stir in enough warm water to make a
smooth, flowing icing. Spoon over the cake, allowing it to flow down
the sides, then leave to set.

easy

serves 8

*prep: 15 minutes +
30 minutes cooling*

40–50 minutes cooking

150 g/5¹/₂ oz butter, plus extra for greasing
115 g/4 oz light muscovado sugar
175 g/6 oz clear honey
1 tbsp water
200 g/7 oz self-raising flour
¹/₂ tsp ground ginger
¹/₂ tsp ground cinnamon
¹/₂ tsp caraway seeds
seeds from 8 cardamom pods, ground
2 eggs, beaten
350 g/12 oz icing sugar

Date & Walnut Teabread

easy

serves 10

prep: 20 minutes +
20 minutes cooling

1 hour–1 hour 15 minutes
cooking

175 g/6 oz butter,
plus extra for greasing
225 g/8 oz stoned dates,
chopped into small pieces
grated rind and juice of 1 orange
50 ml/2 fl oz water
175 g/6 oz light muscovado sugar
3 eggs, beaten
85 g/3 oz wholemeal
self-raising flour
85 g/3 oz white self-raising flour
55 g/2 oz chopped walnuts
8 walnut halves

TO DECORATE
orange zest

Preheat the oven to 160°C/325°F/Gas Mark 3. Grease and line the base and ends of a 900-g/2-lb loaf tin. Place the dates in a saucepan with the orange rind and juice and water and cook over a medium heat for 5 minutes, stirring, or until it is a soft purée.

Place the butter and sugar in a bowl and beat together until light and fluffy. Gradually beat in the eggs, then sift in the flours and fold in with the chopped walnuts. Spread one-third of the mixture over the base of the prepared loaf tin and spread half the date purée over the top.

Repeat the layers, ending with the cake mixture. Arrange walnut halves on top. Bake in the preheated oven for 1–1¼ hours, or until well risen and firm to the touch. Leave to cool in the tin for 10 minutes. Turn out, peel off the lining paper and transfer to a wire rack to cool. Decorate with orange zest and serve in slices.

Banana & Cranberry Loaf

easy

serves 10

prep: 20 minutes

1 hour cooking

1 tbsp butter, for greasing
175 g/6 oz self-raising flour
$^1/_2$ tsp baking powder
150 g/5$^1/_2$ oz soft brown sugar
2 bananas, mashed
50 g/1$^3/_4$ oz chopped mixed peel
25 g/1 oz chopped mixed nuts
50 g/1$^3/_4$ oz dried cranberries
5–6 tbsp orange juice
2 eggs, lightly beaten
150 ml/5 fl oz sunflower oil
75 g/2$^3/_4$ oz icing sugar, sifted
grated rind of 1 orange

Preheat the oven to 180°C/350°F/Gas Mark 4. Grease a 900-g/2-lb loaf tin with the butter and line the base with baking parchment.

Sift the flour and baking powder into a mixing bowl. Stir in the sugar, bananas, chopped mixed peel, nuts and dried cranberries.

In a separate bowl, mix the orange juice, eggs and oil until well blended. Add the mixture to the dry ingredients and mix well. Spoon the mixture into the prepared tin and level the surface with a palette knife.

Bake in the preheated oven for about 1 hour, until firm to the touch or until a fine metal skewer inserted into the centre of the loaf comes out clean. Turn out the loaf onto a wire rack and leave to cool.

Mix the icing sugar with a little water and drizzle the icing over the loaf. Sprinkle the orange rind over the top. Leave the icing to set before serving the loaf in slices.

Marbled Chocolate & Orange Teabread

quite easy

serves 12

prep: 20 minutes +
20 minutes cooling

35–40 minutes cooking

150 g/5¹/₂ oz butter, softened, plus extra for greasing
75 g/2³/₄ oz plain chocolate, broken into pieces
250 g/9 oz golden caster sugar
5 large eggs, beaten
150 g/5¹/₂ oz plain flour
2 tsp baking powder
pinch of salt
grated rind of 2 oranges

Preheat the oven to 180°C/350°F/Gas Mark 4. Grease and line the base and ends of 2 x 450-g/1-lb loaf tins. Place the chocolate in a bowl set over a saucepan of simmering water, making sure that the base of the bowl does not touch the water. Remove from the heat once the chocolate has melted.

Place the butter and sugar in a separate bowl and beat until light and fluffy. Gradually beat in the eggs. Sift the flour, baking powder and salt into the mixture and fold in.

Transfer one-third of the mixture to the melted chocolate and stir together. Stir the orange rind into the remaining mixture and place one-quarter of the mixture in each cake tin, spread in an even layer. Drop spoonfuls of the chocolate mixture on top, dividing it between the 2 tins, but do not smooth it out. Divide the remaining orange mixture between the 2 tins, then, using a knife, gently swirl the top 2 layers together to give a marbled effect.

Bake in the preheated oven for 35–40 minutes, or until a skewer inserted into the centre comes out clean. Leave to cool in the tins for 10 minutes, then turn out, peel off the lining paper and transfer to a wire rack to cool completely.

Sticky Ginger Marmalade Loaf

easy

serves 10

**prep: 10 minutes +
10 minutes cooling**

1 hour cooking

175 g/6 oz butter, softened,
plus extra for greasing
125 g/4^1/2 oz ginger marmalade
175 g/6 oz light muscovado sugar
3 eggs, beaten
225 g/8 oz self-raising flour
^{1}/2 tsp baking powder
1 tsp ground ginger
100 g/3^1/2 oz pecan nuts,
roughly chopped

Preheat the oven to 180°C/350°F/Gas Mark 4. Grease and line the base and ends of a 900-g/2-lb loaf tin. Place 1 tablespoon of the ginger marmalade in a small saucepan and reserve. Place the remaining marmalade in a bowl with the butter, sugar and eggs.

Sift in the flour, baking powder and ground ginger and beat together until smooth. Stir in three-quarters of the nuts. Spoon the mixture into the prepared loaf tin and smooth the top. Sprinkle with the remaining nuts and bake in the preheated oven for 1 hour, or until well risen and a skewer inserted into the centre comes out clean.

Leave to cool in the tin for 10 minutes, then turn out and peel off the lining paper. Transfer to a wire rack to cool until warm. Set the saucepan of reserved marmalade over a low heat to warm, then brush over the loaf and serve in slices.

Sticky Date Cake

quite easy

serves 8

prep: 20 minutes +
30 minutes cooling

1 hour–1 hour 15 minutes
cooking

225 g/8 oz stoned dates, chopped
300 ml/10 fl oz boiling water
115 g/4 oz butter, softened,
plus extra for greasing
175 g/6 oz golden caster sugar
3 eggs, beaten
225 g/8 oz self-raising flour, sifted
$^1/_2$ tsp ground cinnamon
1 tsp bicarbonate of soda

TOPPING

85 g/3 oz light muscovado sugar
55 g/2 oz butter
3 tbsp double cream

Place the dates in a bowl and cover them with the boiling water. Preheat the oven to 180°C/ 350°F/Gas Mark 4, then grease a 23-cm/9-inch round cake tin. Place the butter and sugar in a bowl and beat until light and fluffy. Gradually beat in the eggs, then fold in the flour and cinnamon.

Add the bicarbonate of soda to the dates and water, then pour onto the creamed mixture. Stir until well mixed. Pour into the prepared tin and bake in the preheated oven for 1–1$^1/_4$ hours, or until well risen and firm to the touch.

Preheat the grill to medium. To make the topping, place the sugar, butter and cream in a saucepan. Set over a low heat, stirring, until the sugar has melted, then bring to the boil and simmer for 3 minutes. Pour over the cake and place the cake under the preheated grill until the topping is bubbling. Leave to cool in the tin until the topping has set, then transfer to a wire rack to cool completely before serving.

Banana & Lime Cake

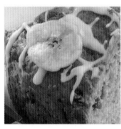

easy

serves 10

prep: 35 minutes +
45 minutes cooling

40–45 minutes cooking

butter, for greasing
300 g/10¹/₂ oz plain flour
1 tsp salt
1¹/₂ tsp baking powder
175 g/6 oz light muscovado sugar
1 tsp grated lime rind
1 egg, beaten
1 banana, mashed with 1 tbsp
lime juice
150 ml/5 fl oz low-fat natural fromage frais
115 g/4 oz sultanas

TOPPING
115 g/4 oz icing sugar
1–2 tsp lime juice
¹/₂ tsp finely grated lime rind

TO DECORATE
banana chips
finely grated lime rind

Preheat the oven to 180°C/350°F/Gas Mark 4. Grease and line a deep 18-cm/7-inch round cake tin with baking parchment. Sift the flour, salt and baking powder into a large bowl and stir in the sugar and lime rind.

Make a well in the centre of the dry ingredients and add the egg, banana, fromage frais and sultanas. Mix well until thoroughly incorporated. Spoon the mixture into the tin and smooth the surface.

Bake in the preheated oven for 40–45 minutes, or until firm to the touch or until a skewer inserted in the centre comes out clean. Leave the cake to cool in the tin for 10 minutes, then turn out onto a wire rack to cool completely.

To make the topping, sift the icing sugar into a small bowl and mix with the lime juice to form a soft, but not too runny icing. Stir in the grated lime rind. Drizzle the icing over the cake, letting it run down the sides. Decorate the cake with banana chips and lime rind. Leave the cake to stand for 15 minutes so that the icing sets.

slices & traybakes

Shortbread Triangles

very easy

makes 8

prep: 20 minutes + cooling

45–50 minutes cooking

115 g/4 oz butter, cut into small pieces, plus extra for greasing
175 g/6 oz plain flour, plus extra for dusting
pinch of salt
55 g/2 oz caster sugar
2 tsp golden caster sugar, for sprinkling

Preheat the oven to 150°C/300°F/Gas Mark 2. Grease a 20-cm/8-inch round fluted cake tin or flan tin.

Mix together the flour, salt and sugar. Rub the butter into the dry ingredients. Continue to work the mixture until it forms a soft dough. Make sure you do not overwork the shortbread or it will be tough, not crumbly as it should be.

Lightly press the dough into the cake tin. If you don't have a fluted tin, roll out the dough on a lightly floured board, place on a baking tray and pinch the edges to form a scalloped pattern.

Mark into 8 pieces with a knife. Prick all over with a fork and bake in the centre of the preheated oven for 45–50 minutes until the shortbread is firm and just coloured.

Allow to cool in the tin and sprinkle with the sugar. Cut into portions and remove to a wire rack. Store in an airtight container in a cool place until needed.

Ginger-Topped Fingers

Preheat the oven to 180°C/350°F/Gas Mark 4. Grease a 28 x 18-cm/ 11 x 7-inch cake tin. Sift the flour and ginger into a bowl and stir in the sugar. Rub in the butter until the mixture begins to stick together.

Press the mixture into the prepared tin and smooth the top with a palette knife. Bake in the preheated oven for 40 minutes, or until very lightly browned.

To make the topping, place the syrup and butter in a small saucepan over a low heat and stir until melted. Stir in the icing sugar and ginger. Remove the shortbread base from the oven and pour the topping over it while both are still hot. Leave to cool slightly in the tin, then cut into 16 fingers. Transfer to wire racks to cool completely.

very easy

makes 16

prep: 15 minutes +
30 minutes cooling

40 minutes cooking

175 g/6 oz butter, plus extra for greasing
225 g/8 oz plain flour
1 tsp ground ginger
85 g/3 oz golden caster sugar

GINGER TOPPING

1 tbsp golden syrup
55 g/2 oz butter
2 tbsp icing sugar
1 tsp ground ginger

Cinnamon & Seed Squares

very easy

makes 12

prep: 10 minutes + 1 hour
cooling

45 minutes cooking

250 g/9 oz butter, softened,
plus extra for greasing
250 g/9 oz caster sugar
3 eggs, beaten
250 g/9 oz self-raising flour
$^1/_2$ tsp bicarbonate of soda
1 tbsp ground cinnamon
150 ml/5 fl oz soured cream
100 g/3$^1/_2$ oz sunflower seeds

Preheat the oven to 180°C/350°F/Gas Mark 4. Grease a 23-cm/9-inch square cake tin and line the base with baking parchment. Beat the butter and caster sugar together in a large bowl until the mixture is light and fluffy. Gradually add the beaten eggs to the mixture, beating thoroughly after each addition.

Sift the self-raising flour, bicarbonate of soda and ground cinnamon into the creamed mixture and fold in gently, using a metal spoon. Spoon in the soured cream and sunflower seeds and gently mix until well combined.

Spoon the mixture into the prepared cake tin and smooth the surface with the back of a spoon or a knife. Bake in the preheated oven for 45 minutes, or until the mixture is firm to the touch when pressed with a finger.

Loosen the edges with a round-bladed knife, then turn out onto a wire rack to cool completely. Slice into 12 squares.

Almond Slices

75 g/2³/₄ oz ground almonds
200 g/7 oz dried milk
200 g/7 oz sugar
¹/₂ tsp saffron threads
100 g/3¹/₂ oz unsalted butter
3 eggs, beaten
flaked almonds, to decorate

Preheat the oven to 160°C/325°F/Gas Mark 3.

Place the ground almonds, dried milk, sugar and saffron in a large mixing bowl and mix well.

Melt the butter in a small saucepan over a low heat. Pour the melted butter over the dry ingredients and mix well until thoroughly blended. Add the beaten eggs and mix well.

Spread the mixture in a shallow 18–23-cm/7–9-inch ovenproof dish and bake in the preheated oven for 45 minutes, or until a fine metal skewer inserted into the centre of the cake comes out clean.

Cut the almond cake into 8 slices. Decorate the almond slices with flaked almonds and transfer to serving plates. Serve hot or cold.

Chocolate Peppermint Slices

easy

makes 16

prep: 15 minutes

10–15 minutes cooking

55 g/2 oz butter, plus extra for greasing

55 g/2 oz caster sugar

115 g/4 oz plain flour

175 g/6 oz icing sugar

1–2 tbsp warm water

$^{1}/_{2}$ tsp peppermint essence

175 g/6 oz dark chocolate,
broken into pieces

Preheat the oven to 180°C/350°F/Gas Mark 4. Grease and line a 20 x 30-cm/8 x 12-inch Swiss roll tin with baking parchment. Whisk the butter and sugar together until pale and fluffy. Stir in the flour until the mixture binds together.

Knead the mixture to form a smooth dough, then press into the prepared tin. Prick the surface all over with a fork. Bake in the preheated oven for 10–15 minutes, until lightly browned and just firm to the touch. Leave to cool in the tin.

Sift the icing sugar into a bowl. Gradually add the water, then add the peppermint essence. Spread the icing over the base, then leave to set.

Melt the chocolate in a heatproof bowl set over a saucepan of gently simmering water, then spread over the peppermint icing. Leave to set, then cut into slices.

Chocolate Caramel Slices

Preheat the oven to 180°C/350°F/Gas Mark 4. Beat together the margarine and brown sugar in a bowl until light and fluffy. Beat in the flour and the rolled oats. Use your fingertips to bring the mixture together, if necessary.

Press the mixture into the base of a shallow 20-cm/8-inch square cake tin.

Bake in the preheated oven for 25 minutes, or until just golden and firm. Cool in the tin.

Place the ingredients for the caramel filling in a saucepan and heat gently, stirring until the sugar has dissolved. Bring slowly to the boil over a very low heat, then boil very gently for 3–4 minutes, stirring constantly, until thickened.

Pour the caramel filling over the oat layer in the tin and leave to set.

Melt the dark chocolate and spread it over the caramel. If using the white chocolate, place in a heatproof bowl set over a saucepan of gently simmering water until melted. Pipe lines of white chocolate over the dark chocolate. Using a cocktail stick, feather the white chocolate into the dark chocolate. Leave to set, then cut into slices to serve.

very easy

makes 16

prep: 40 minutes

25 minutes cooking

75 g/2³/₄ oz soft margarine
60 g/2¹/₄ oz soft brown sugar
140 g/5 oz plain flour
40 g/1¹/₂ oz rolled oats

CARAMEL FILLING
2 tbsp butter
2 tbsp soft brown sugar
225 ml/8 fl oz condensed milk

TOPPING
100 g/3¹/₂ oz dark chocolate
25 g/1 oz white chocolate (optional)

Coconut & Cherry Flapjacks

very easy

makes 16

prep: 15 minutes +
30 minutes cooling

30 minutes cooking

200 g/7 oz butter, plus extra
for greasing
200 g/7 oz demerara sugar
2 tbsp golden syrup
275 g/9¹/₂ oz rolled oats
100 g/3¹/₂ oz desiccated coconut
75 g/2³/₄ oz glacé cherries,
chopped

Preheat the oven to 160°C/325°F/Gas Mark 3, then grease a 30 x 23-cm/12 x 9-inch baking tray.

Heat the butter, sugar and syrup in a large saucepan over a low heat until just melted. Stir in the oats, coconut and cherries and mix until evenly combined.

Spread the mixture evenly on to the baking tray and press down with the back of a spatula to make a smooth surface.

Bake in the preheated oven for 30 minutes. Remove from the oven and leave to cool on the baking tray for 10 minutes. Cut the flapjack into rectangles using a sharp knife. Carefully transfer the pieces to a wire rack and leave to cool completely.

Nutty Flapjacks

very easy

makes 16

**prep: 10 minutes +
30 minutes cooling**

20–25 minutes cooking

115 g/4 oz butter, plus extra
for greasing
200 g/7 oz rolled oats
115 g/4 oz chopped hazelnuts
55 g/2 oz plain flour
2 tbsp golden syrup
85 g/3 oz light muscovado sugar

Preheat the oven to 180°C/350°F/Gas Mark 4, then grease a 23-cm/9-inch square ovenproof dish or cake tin. Place the rolled oats, chopped hazelnuts and flour in a large mixing bowl and stir together.

Place the butter, syrup and sugar in a saucepan over a low heat and stir until melted. Pour on to the dry ingredients and mix well. Turn the mixture into the prepared ovenproof dish and smooth the surface with the back of a spoon.

Bake in the preheated oven for 20–25 minutes, or until golden and firm to the touch. Mark into 16 pieces and leave to cool in the tin. When completely cold, cut through with a sharp knife and remove from the tin.

Chocolate Marshmallow Fingers

very easy

makes 18

prep: 10 minutes +
2-3 hours chilling

0 minutes cooking

350 g/12 oz digestive biscuits
125 g/4¹/₂ oz dark chocolate,
broken into pieces
225 g/8 oz butter
25 g/1 oz caster sugar
2 tbsp cocoa powder
2 tbsp honey
55 g/2 oz mini marshmallows
100 g/3¹/₂ oz white chocolate chips

Put the digestive biscuits in a polythene bag and, using a rolling pin, crush into small pieces.

Put the chocolate, butter, sugar, cocoa and honey in a saucepan and heat gently until melted. Remove from the heat and leave to cool slightly.

Stir the crushed biscuits into the chocolate mixture until well mixed. Add the marshmallows and mix well, then finally stir in the chocolate chips.

Turn the mixture into a 20-cm/8-inch square cake tin and lightly smooth the top. Put in the refrigerator and leave to chill for 2–3 hours, until set. Cut into fingers before serving.

Chocolate Slab Cake

Preheat the oven to 190°C/375°F/Gas Mark 5. Grease a 33 x 20-cm/ 13 x 8-inch cake tin and line the base with baking parchment. Melt the butter and chocolate with the water in a saucepan over a low heat, stirring frequently.

Sift the flour and baking powder into a mixing bowl and stir in the sugar.

Pour the hot chocolate liquid into the bowl and then beat well until all of the ingredients are evenly mixed. Stir in the soured cream, followed by the eggs.

Pour the mixture into the cake tin and bake in the preheated oven for 40–45 minutes, until springy to the touch.

Leave the cake to cool slightly in the tin before turning it out onto a wire rack. Leave to cool completely.

To make the icing, melt the chocolate with the water in a saucepan over a very low heat, stir in the cream and remove from the heat. Stir in the chilled butter, then pour the icing over the cooled cake, using a palette knife to spread it evenly over the top of the cake.

very easy

serves 4

prep: 55 minutes

40–45 minutes cooking

200 g/7 oz butter, plus extra for greasing
100 g/3^{1}/$_{2}$ oz continental dark
chocolate, broken into pieces
75 ml/2^{1}/$_{2}$ fl oz water
350 g/12 oz plain flour
2 tsp baking powder
250 g/9 oz soft light brown sugar
75 ml/2^{1}/$_{2}$ fl oz soured cream
2 eggs, beaten

ICING
200 g/7 oz dark chocolate
6 tbsp water
3 tbsp single cream
1 tbsp butter, chilled

Walnut & Cinnamon Blondies

easy

makes 9

*prep: 10 minutes +
30 minutes cooling*

20–25 minutes cooking

*115 g/4 oz butter, plus extra
for greasing*
225 g/8 oz light muscovado sugar
1 egg
1 egg yolk
140 g/5 oz self-raising flour
1 tsp ground cinnamon
85 g/3 oz walnuts, roughly chopped

Preheat the oven to 180°C/350°F/Gas Mark 4. Grease and line the base of an 18-cm/7-inch square cake tin.

Place the butter and sugar in a saucepan over a low heat and stir until the sugar has dissolved. Cook, stirring, for a further minute. The mixture will bubble slightly, but do not let it boil. Leave to cool for 10 minutes.

Stir the egg and egg yolk into the mixture. Sift in the flour and cinnamon, add the nuts and stir until just blended. Pour the cake mixture into the prepared tin, then bake in the preheated oven for 20–25 minutes, or until springy in the centre and a skewer inserted into the centre of the cake comes out clean.

Leave to cool in the tin for a few minutes, then run a knife around the edge of the cake to loosen it. Turn the cake out onto a wire rack and peel off the lining paper. Leave to cool completely. When cold, cut into squares.

Gingerbread

easy

makes 12

prep: 15 minutes

30-35 minutes cooking

150 g/5¹/₂ oz butter, plus extra
for greasing
175 g/6 oz soft brown sugar
2 tbsp black treacle
225 g/8 oz plain flour
1 tsp baking powder
2 tsp bicarbonate of soda
2 tsp ground ginger
150 ml/5 fl oz milk
1 egg, beaten
2 eating apples, peeled, chopped,
and coated with lemon juice to
prevent them browning

Preheat the oven to 160°C/325°F/Gas Mark 3. Grease a 23-cm/9-inch square cake tin with a little butter and line with baking paper.

Melt the butter, sugar and treacle in a saucepan over a low heat, then leave the mixture to cool.

Sift the flour, baking powder, bicarbonate of soda and ground ginger into a mixing bowl.
Stir in the milk, beaten egg and cooled butter and treacle mixture, followed by the chopped apples.
Stir together gently, then pour the mixture into the prepared tin and level the surface with a palette knife.

Bake in the preheated oven for 30–35 minutes, until the cake has risen and a fine metal skewer inserted into the centre comes out clean.

Leave the ginger cake to cool in the tin, then turn out and cut into 12 bars.

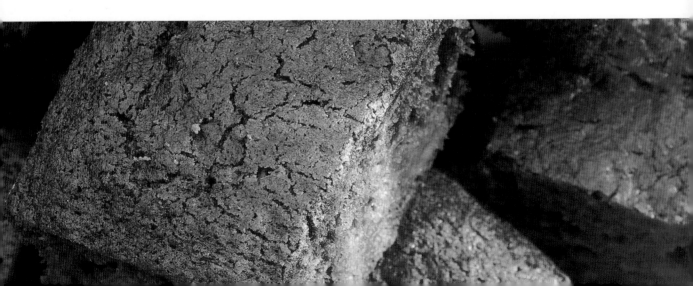

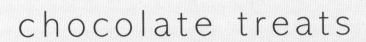

chocolate treats

Chocolate Brownies

very easy

serves 4

prep: 20 minutes +
1-2 hours to cool/set

30 minutes cooking

225 g/8 oz butter, diced, plus extra for greasing
150 g/5¹/₂ oz dark chocolate, chopped
225 g/8 oz self-raising flour
125 g/4¹/₂ oz dark muscovado sugar
4 eggs, beaten
60 g/2¹/₄ oz blanched hazelnuts, chopped
60 g/2¹/₄ oz sultanas
100 g/3¹/₂ oz dark chocolate chips

TO DECORATE

115 g/4 oz white chocolate, melted

Preheat the oven to 180°C/350°F/Gas Mark 4. Grease and line a 28 x 18-cm/11 x 7-inch rectangular cake tin.

Put the butter and dark chocolate pieces into a heatproof bowl and set over a saucepan of simmering water until melted. Remove from the heat. Sift the flour into a large bowl, add the sugar and mix well. Stir the eggs into the chocolate mixture, then beat into the flour mixture. Add the nuts, sultanas and chocolate chips and mix well. Spoon evenly into the cake tin and level the surface.

Bake in the preheated oven for 30 minutes, or until firm. To check whether the cake is cooked through, insert a skewer into the centre – it should come out clean. If not, return the cake to the oven for a few minutes. Remove from the oven and leave to cool for 15 minutes. Turn out onto a wire rack to cool completely. To decorate, drizzle the melted white chocolate in fine lines over the cake, then cut into bars. Leave to set before serving.

Ginger Chocolate Chip Squares

Preheat the oven to 150°C/300°F/Gas Mark 2. Finely chop the stem ginger. Sift the flour, ground ginger, cinnamon, cloves and nutmeg into a large bowl. Stir in the chopped stem ginger and sugar.

Put the butter and the syrup into a saucepan and heat gently until melted. Bring to the boil, then pour into the flour mixture, stirring all the time. Beat until the mixture is cool enough to handle.

Add the chocolate chips to the mixture. Press evenly into a 20 x 30-cm/ 8 x 12-inch Swiss roll tin.

Transfer to the preheated oven and bake for 30 minutes. Cut into squares, then leave to cool in the tin.

very easy

makes 15

prep: 10 minutes

30 minutes cooking

4 pieces stem ginger in syrup
225 g/8 oz plain flour
1 $^{1}/_{2}$ tsp ground ginger
1 tsp ground cinnamon
$^{1}/_{4}$ tsp ground cloves
$^{1}/_{4}$ tsp grated nutmeg
115 g/4 oz soft brown sugar
115 g/4 oz butter
115 g/4 oz golden syrup
100 g/3$^{1}/_{2}$ oz dark chocolate chips

Chocolate Temptations

very easy

makes 24

prep: 15-20 minutes

15 minutes cooking

90 g/3¹/₄ oz unsalted butter,
plus extra for greasing
365 g/12¹/₂ oz dark chocolate
1 tsp strong coffee
2 eggs
140 g/5 oz soft brown sugar
185 g/6¹/₂ oz plain flour
¹/₄ tsp baking powder
pinch of salt
2 tsp almond essence
85 g/3 oz chopped Brazil nuts
85 g/3 oz chopped hazelnuts
40 g/1¹/₂ oz white chocolate

Preheat the oven to 180°C/350°F/Gas Mark 4. Grease a large baking sheet. Put 225 g/8 oz of the dark chocolate with the butter and coffee into a heatproof bowl set over a saucepan of gently simmering water and heat until the chocolate is almost melted.

Meanwhile, beat the eggs in a bowl until fluffy. Whisk in the sugar gradually until thick. Remove the chocolate from the heat and stir until smooth. Add to the egg mixture and stir until combined.

Sift the flour, baking powder and salt into a bowl and stir into the chocolate mixture. Chop 85 g/3 oz of the remaining dark chocolate into pieces and stir into the mixture. Stir in the almond essence and chopped nuts.

Put 24 tablespoonfuls of the mixture on to the baking sheet, transfer to the preheated oven and bake for 15 minutes. Transfer the biscuits to a wire rack to cool. To decorate, melt the remaining chocolate (dark and white) in turn, then spoon into a piping bag and pipe lines on to the biscuits.

Chocolate Chip Cookies

very easy

serves 4

prep: 15 minutes +
cooling

12–15 minutes cooking

*125 g/4¹/₂ oz butter, softened,
plus extra for greasing
125 g/4¹/₂ oz dark muscovado sugar
1 egg, beaten
190 g/6¹/₂ oz self-raising flour
2 tbsp unsweetened cocoa powder
1 tsp almond extract
120 g/4¹/₄ oz dark chocolate chips
55 g/2 oz shelled mixed nuts,
chopped*

Preheat the oven to 190°C/375°F/Gas Mark 5. Grease two large baking trays.

Put the butter and sugar into a large bowl and cream until fluffy. Gradually beat in the egg. Sift the flour and cocoa powder into a separate bowl, then fold into the egg mixture with the almond extract. Stir in the chocolate chips and nuts. Drop rounded dessertspoonfuls of the mixture on to the prepared baking trays, leaving plenty of space between them to allow them to spread during cooking.

Bake in the preheated oven for 12–15 minutes, or until golden. Remove from the oven, transfer to wire racks and leave to cool completely. Store in an airtight tin until ready to serve.

Double Chocolate Muffins

easy

makes 12

prep: 15 minutes + cooling

20 minutes cooking

200 g/7 oz plain flour
25 g/1 oz cocoa powder, plus extra for dusting
1 tbsp baking powder
1 tsp ground cinnamon
115 g/4 oz golden caster sugar
185 g/6^1/$_2$ oz white chocolate, broken into pieces
2 large eggs
100 ml/3^1/$_2$ fl oz sunflower or peanut oil
200 ml/7 fl oz milk

Preheat the oven to 200°C/400°F/Gas Mark 6. Line a 12-cup muffin tin with muffin paper cases.

Sift the flour, cocoa, baking powder and cinnamon into a large mixing bowl. Stir in the sugar and 125 g/4^1/$_2$ oz of the white chocolate.

Place the eggs and oil in a separate bowl and whisk until frothy, then gradually whisk in the milk. Stir into the dry ingredients until just blended. Divide the mixture evenly between the paper cases, filling each three-quarters full. Bake in the preheated oven for 20 minutes or until well risen and springy to the touch. Remove the muffins from the oven, cool in the tin for 2 minutes, then transfer to a wire rack to cool completely.

Place the remaining white chocolate in a heatproof bowl, set the bowl over a saucepan of barely simmering water, and heat until melted. Spread over the top of the muffins. Allow to set, then dust the tops with a little cocoa and serve.

Chocolate Pistachio Biscuits

easy

makes 24

prep: 25 minutes +
30 minutes cooling

30 minutes cooking

2 tbsp butter, unsalted for preference,
plus extra for greasing
175 g/6 oz dark chocolate,
broken into pieces
350 g/12 oz self-raising flour,
plus extra for dusting
1 $^1/_2$ tsp baking powder
85 g/3 oz caster sugar
70 g/2 $^1/_2$ oz cornmeal
finely grated rind of 1 lemon
2 tsp Amaretto
1 egg, beaten lightly
115 g/4 oz coarsely chopped
pistachio nuts
2 tbsp icing sugar, for dusting

Preheat the oven to 160°C/325°F/Gas Mark 3. Grease a baking sheet with butter. Put the chocolate and 2 tablespoons of butter in a heatproof bowl set over a saucepan of gently simmering water. Stir over a low heat until melted and smooth. Remove from the heat and cool slightly.

Sift the flour and baking powder into a bowl and mix in the caster sugar, cornmeal, lemon rind, Amaretto, egg and pistachio nuts. Stir in the chocolate mixture and mix to a soft dough.

Lightly dust your hands with flour, divide the dough in half and shape each piece into a 28-cm/11-inch long cylinder. Transfer the cylinders to the prepared baking sheet and flatten, with the palm of your hand, to about 2 cm/$^3/_4$ inch thick. Bake the biscuits in the preheated oven for about 20 minutes, until firm to the touch.

Remove the baking sheet from the oven and leave the cooked pieces to cool. When cool, put the cooked pieces on a cutting board and slice them diagonally into thin biscuits. Return them to the baking sheet and bake for a further 10 minutes, until crisp. Remove from the oven and transfer to a wire rack to cool. Dust lightly with icing sugar.

White Chocolate Cake

easy

serves 4-6

prep: 30 minutes +
cooling/chilling overnight

20 minutes cooking

butter, for greasing
4 eggs
125 g/4¹/₂ oz caster sugar
125 g/4¹/₂ oz plain flour, sifted
pinch of salt
300 ml/10 fl oz double cream
150 g/5¹/₂ oz white chocolate,
chopped

CHOCOLATE LEAVES
75 g/2³/₄ oz dark or white
chocolate, melted
handful of rose leaves, or
other small edible leaves with
well-defined veins, washed
and dried

To make the leaves, brush the melted chocolate over the bottom of the leaves. Arrange, coated sides up, on a baking sheet lined with baking parchment. Chill until set, then peel away the leaves.

Preheat the oven to 180°C/350°F/Gas Mark 4. Grease and line a 20-cm/8-inch round cake tin. Put the eggs and sugar into a heatproof bowl and set over a saucepan of simmering water. Whisk until thick, remove from the heat and whisk until cool. Fold in the flour and salt. Pour into the tin and bake in the preheated oven for 20 minutes, then cool for 10 minutes. Turn out, discard the lining paper and leave to cool.

Put the cream into a saucepan over a low heat and bring to the boil, stirring. Add the chocolate and stir until melted. Pour into a bowl, cover with clingfilm and chill overnight.

Cut the cake horizontally in half. Whisk the cream until thick, spread one-third over one half of the cake and top with the other, then coat with the remaining cream. Chill for 1–2 hours, decorate with the chocolate leaves and serve.

Chocolate Cake with Syrup

very easy

serves 12

prep: 15 minutes

35 minutes cooking

115 g/4 oz unsalted butter,
plus extra for greasing
225 g/8 oz dark chocolate,
broken into pieces
1 tbsp strong black coffee
4 large eggs
2 egg yolks
115 g/4 oz golden caster sugar
40 g/1¹/₂ oz plain flour
2 tsp ground cinnamon
85 g/3 oz ground almonds

TO DECORATE

chocolate-covered coffee beans,

SYRUP

300 ml/10 fl oz strong black coffee
115 g/4 oz golden caster sugar
1 cinnamon stick

Preheat the oven to 190°C/375°F/Gas Mark 5. Grease and line the base of a deep 20-cm/8-inch round cake tin. Place the chocolate, butter and coffee in a heatproof bowl and set over a saucepan of gently simmering water until melted. Stir to blend, then remove from the heat and leave to cool slightly.

Place the whole eggs, egg yolks and sugar in a separate bowl and whisk together until thick and pale. Sift the flour and cinnamon over the egg mixture. Add the almonds and the chocolate mixture and fold in carefully. Spoon the mixture into the prepared tin. Bake in the preheated oven for 35 minutes, or until the tip of a knife inserted into the centre comes out clean. Leave to cool slightly before turning out onto a serving plate.

Meanwhile, make the syrup. Place the coffee, sugar and cinnamon stick in a heavy-based saucepan and heat gently, stirring, until the sugar has dissolved. Increase the heat and boil for 5 minutes, or until reduced and thickened slightly. Keep warm. Pierce the surface of the cake with a cocktail stick, then drizzle over half the coffee syrup. Decorate with chocolate-covered coffee beans and serve, cut into wedges, with the remaining coffee syrup.

Chocolate Fudge Gateau

Preheat the oven to 180°C/350°F/Gas Mark 4. Lightly oil and line the base of 2 x 20-cm/8-inch shallow, round cake tins with baking parchment. Melt the chocolate in a heatproof bowl set over a saucepan of gently simmering water. Cream the butter and sugar together until light and fluffy, then gradually add the eggs, beating well between each addition and adding a little flour after each addition. When all the eggs have been added, stir in the melted chocolate and then the remaining flour and mix lightly together.

Stir in the ground almonds together with 1–2 tablespoons of cooled boiled water. Mix to form a soft dropping consistency. Stir in the fudge pieces, then divide between the prepared cake tins and smooth the tops. Bake in the preheated oven for 35–40 minutes, or until the tops spring back when touched lightly with a finger. Remove and leave to cool before turning out onto wire racks and discarding the lining paper. Leave until cold.

Beat the butter for the icing until soft and creamy, then gradually beat in the icing sugar, adding a little cream as the mixture becomes stiff. Add the muscovado sugar with the cocoa and stir lightly. Stir in sufficient of the remaining cream to give a soft spreadable icing.

Place the grated chocolate on a sheet of baking parchment. Split the cakes in half horizontally and sandwich together with a third of the prepared icing. Spread another third around the sides, then roll the cake in the grated chocolate. Place on a serving plate. Spread the top with the remaining icing, piping rosettes around the outside edge for an attractive finish. Decorate with the truffles before serving the gateau.

easy

serves 10

prep: 20 minutes

35–40 minutes cooking

1 tsp sunflower oil, for oiling
85 g/3 oz dark chocolate
225 g/8 oz butter, softened
225 g/8 oz light muscovado sugar
4 eggs, beaten
225 g/8 oz self-raising flour
55 g/2 oz ground almonds
115 g/4 oz soft vanilla fudge, finely chopped

ICING

175 g/6 oz butter, softened
280 g/10 oz icing sugar, sifted
3–4 tbsp single cream
55 g/2 oz light muscovado sugar
1 tbsp cocoa powder, sifted

TO DECORATE

55 g/2 oz dark chocolate, grated
cocoa-dusted truffles

Chocolate Banana Loaf

easy

serves 4-6

prep: 15 minutes

1 hour cooking

115 g/4 oz butter, softened,
plus extra for greasing
200 g/7 oz soft brown sugar
2 eggs
3 bananas
225 g/8 oz plain flour
1 tsp bicarbonate of soda
1 tbsp unsweetened cocoa powder
1 tsp mixed spice
125 ml/4 fl oz thick natural yogurt
85 g/3 oz dark chocolate chips

Preheat the oven to 180°C/350°F/Gas Mark 4. Grease a 23 x 13 x 7.5-cm/9 x 5 x 3-inch loaf tin.

Put the butter, sugar and eggs into a bowl and beat well. Peel and mash the bananas, then add to the mixture. Stir in well. Sift the flour, bicarbonate of soda, cocoa powder and mixed spice into a separate bowl, then add to the banana mixture and mix well. Stir in the yogurt and chocolate chips. Spoon the mixture into the prepared tin and level the surface.

Bake in the preheated oven for 1 hour. To test whether the loaf is cooked through, insert a cocktail stick into the centre – it should come out clean. If not, return the loaf to the oven for a few minutes.

Deep Chocolate Cheesecake

very easy

serves 4–6

prep: 15–20 minutes +
4 hours chilling

0 min cooking

BASE

*4 tbsp butter, melted,
plus extra for greasing
115 g/4 oz digestive biscuits,
finely crushed
2 tsp unsweetened cocoa powder*

CHOCOLATE LAYER

*800 g/1 lb 12 oz mascarpone
cheese
200 g/7 oz icing sugar, sifted
juice of $^1/_2$ orange
finely grated rind of 1 orange
175 g/6 oz dark chocolate, melted
2 tbsp brandy*

TO DECORATE

*chocolate leaves (see page 65)
halved kumquats*

Grease a 20-cm/8-inch loose-bottomed, round cake tin.

To make the base, put the crushed biscuits, cocoa powder and melted butter into a large bowl and mix well. Press the biscuit mixture evenly over the base of the prepared tin.

Put the mascarpone and sugar into a bowl and stir in the orange juice and rind. Add the melted chocolate and brandy, and mix together until thoroughly combined. Spread the chocolate mixture evenly over the biscuit layer. Cover with clingfilm and chill for at least 4 hours.

Remove the cheesecake from the refrigerator, turn out onto a serving platter and decorate with chocolate leaves and kumquat halves. Serve immediately.

Chocolate Cherry Gateau

easy

serves 8

prep: 15 minutes +
30 minutes cooling

40 minutes cooking

3 tbsp unsalted butter, melted, plus extra for greasing
450 g/1 lb fresh cherries, stoned and halved
250 g/9 oz caster sugar
100 ml/3¹/₂ fl oz cherry brandy
100 g/3¹/₂ oz plain flour
50g/1³/₄ oz cocoa powder
¹/₂ tsp baking powder
4 eggs
700 ml/1¹/₄ pints double cream

TO DECORATE
grated dark chocolate and whole fresh cherries

Preheat the oven to 180°C/350°F/Gas Mark 4. Grease and line a 23-cm/9-inch round cake tin. Put the cherries into a saucepan, add 3 tablespoons of the sugar and the cherry brandy. Simmer for 5 minutes. Drain, reserving the syrup. In another bowl, sift together the flour, cocoa and baking powder.

Put the eggs in a heatproof bowl and beat in 160 g/5³/₄ oz of the sugar. Place the bowl over a pan of simmering water and beat for 6 minutes or until thickened. Remove from the heat, then gradually fold in the flour mixture and melted butter. Spoon into the cake tin. Bake in the preheated oven for 40 minutes. Remove from the oven and leave to cool.

Turn out the cake and cut in half horizontally. Mix the cream with the remaining sugar and whip to soft peaks. Spread the reserved syrup over the cut sides of the cake. Arrange the cherries over one half, top with a layer of cream, and place the other half on top. Cover the top of the cake with cream, sprinkle with grated chocolate and decorate with cherries.

Chocolate Truffle Cake

Preheat the oven to 180°C/350°F/Gas Mark 4. Lightly grease and line the base of a 20-cm/8-inch round springform tin. Beat the butter and sugar together until light and fluffy. Gradually add the eggs, beating well after each addition.

Sift the flour, baking powder and cocoa together and fold into the cake mixture along with the ground almonds. Pour into the prepared tin and bake in the preheated oven for 20–25 minutes, or until springy to the touch. Leave the cake to cool slightly in the tin, then transfer to a wire rack to cool completely. Wash and dry the tin and return the cooled cake to the tin.

To make the topping, heat the chocolate, butter and cream in a heavy-based saucepan over a low heat and stir until smooth. Cool, then chill for 30 minutes. Beat well with a wooden spoon and chill for a further 30 minutes. Beat the mixture again, then add the cake crumbs and rum, beating until well combined. Spoon over the sponge cake and leave to chill for 3 hours.

Meanwhile, put the chocolate in a heatproof bowl set over a saucepan of gently simmering water until melted. Dip the cape gooseberries in the melted chocolate until partially covered. Leave to set on baking parchment. Transfer the cake to a serving plate and decorate with the cape gooseberries.

very easy

serves 12

prep: 45 minutes +
4 hours chilling

20–25 minutes cooking

75 g/2³/₄ oz butter plus extra for greasing
75 g/2³/₄ oz caster sugar
2 eggs, lightly beaten
75 g/2³/₄ oz self-raising flour
¹/₂ tsp baking powder
85 g/3 oz cocoa powder
50 g/1³/₄ oz ground almonds

TRUFFLE TOPPING
350 g/12 oz dark chocolate
115 g/4 oz butter
300 ml/10 fl oz double cream
70 g/2¹/₂ oz plain cake crumbs
3 tbsp dark rum

TO DECORATE
50 g/1³/₄ oz dark chocolate, broken into pieces
cape gooseberries

small bites

Lavender Fairy Cakes

very easy

makes 12

prep: 15 minutes +
20 minutes cooling

12–15 minutes cooking

115 g/4 oz golden caster sugar
115 g/4 oz butter, softened
2 eggs, beaten
1 tbsp milk
1 tsp finely chopped lavender flowers
$^1/_2$ tsp vanilla essence
175 g/6 oz self-raising flour, sifted
140 g/5 oz icing sugar

TO DECORATE
lavender flowers
silver dragées

Preheat the preheated oven to 200°C/400°F/Gas Mark 6. Place 12 paper cake cases in a bun tin. Place the caster sugar and butter in a bowl and cream together until pale and fluffy. Gradually beat in the eggs. Stir in the milk, lavender and vanilla essence, then carefully fold in the flour.

Divide the mixture between the paper cases and bake in the preheated oven for 12–15 minutes, or until well risen and golden. The sponge should bounce back when pressed. A few minutes before the cakes are ready, sift the icing sugar into a bowl and stir in enough water to make a thick icing.

When the cakes are baked, transfer to a wire rack and place a blob of icing in the centre of each one, allowing it to run across the cake. Decorate with lavender flowers and silver dragées and serve as soon as the cakes are cool.

Chocolate Butterfly Cakes

easy

makes 12

prep: 30 minutes

15 minutes cooking

115 g/4 oz soft margarine
100 g/3¹/₂ oz caster sugar
225 g/8 oz self-raising flour
2 large eggs
2 tbsp cocoa powder
25 g/1 oz dark chocolate, melted
icing sugar, for dusting

LEMON BUTTERCREAM
85 g/3 oz butter, unsalted for
preference, softened
150 g/5¹/₂ oz icing sugar, sifted
grated rind of ¹/₂ lemon
1 tbsp lemon juice

Preheat the oven to 180°C/350°F/Gas Mark 4. Line a shallow muffin tin with 12 muffin paper cases. Place all of the ingredients for the cakes, except the chocolate and icing sugar, in a large bowl, and beat with an electric whisk until the mixture is just smooth. Beat in the melted chocolate.

Spoon equal amounts of the mixture into each paper case, filling them three-quarters full. Bake in the preheated oven for 15 minutes, or until springy to the touch. Transfer to a wire rack and leave to cool.

Meanwhile, make the lemon buttercream. Place the butter in a mixing bowl and beat until fluffy, then gradually beat in the icing sugar. Beat in the lemon rind and gradually add the lemon juice, beating well.

When cold, cut the top off each cake, using a serrated knife. Cut each cake top in half.

Spread or pipe the buttercream icing over the cut surface of each cake and push the 2 cut pieces of cake top into the icing to form wings. Dust with icing sugar.

Chocolate Cupcakes

easy

makes 18

prep: 20 minutes +
1 hour chilling

20 minutes cooking

85 g/3 oz butter, softened
100 g/3¹/₂ oz caster sugar
2 eggs, lightly beaten
2 tbsp milk
55 g/2 oz dark chocolate chips
225 g/8 oz self-raising flour
25 g/1 oz cocoa powder

ICING
225 g/8 oz white chocolate
150 g/5¹/₂ oz low-fat cream cheese

Preheat the oven to 200°C/400°F/Gas Mark 6. Line a shallow muffin tin with 18 muffin paper cases.

Beat together the butter and sugar until pale and fluffy. Gradually add the eggs, beating well after each addition. Add a little of the flour if the mixture starts to curdle. Add the milk, then fold in the chocolate chips.

Sift together the flour and cocoa and fold into the mixture with a metal spoon or palette knife. Divide the batter equally between the muffin paper cases and smooth the tops.

Bake in the preheated oven for 20 minutes, or until well risen and springy to the touch. Cool on a wire rack.

To make the icing, melt the chocolate in a heatproof bowl set over a saucepan of gently simmering water. Cool slightly. Beat the cream cheese until softened, then beat in the chocolate. Spread a little of the icing over each cake and leave to chill for 1 hour before serving.

Low-fat Blueberry Muffins

Preheat the oven to 190°C/375°F/Gas Mark 5. Spray a 12-cup muffin tin with vegetable oil cooking spray, or line it with 12 muffin paper cases.

Sift the flour, bicarbonate of soda, salt and half of the allspice into a large mixing bowl. Add 6 tablespoons of the caster sugar and mix together.

In a separate bowl, whisk the egg whites together. Add the margarine, yogurt and vanilla essence and mix together well, then stir in the fresh blueberries until thoroughly mixed. Add the fruit mixture to the flour mixture, then gently stir until just combined. Do not overstir the mixture – it is fine for it to be a little lumpy.

Divide the muffin mixture evenly between the 12 cups in the muffin tin or the paper cases (they should be about two-thirds full). Mix the remaining sugar with the remaining allspice, then sprinkle the mixture over the muffins. Transfer to the preheated oven and bake for 25 minutes or until risen and golden. Remove the muffins from the oven and serve warm, or place them on a wire rack to cool.

very easy

makes 12

prep: 15 minutes +
cooling

25 minutes cooking

vegetable oil cooking spray, for oiling (if using)
225 g/8 oz plain flour
1 tsp bicarbonate of soda
$^{1}/_{4}$ tsp salt
1 tsp allspice
115 g/4 oz caster sugar
3 egg whites
3 tbsp low-fat margarine
150 ml/5 fl oz thick low-fat natural or blueberry-flavoured yogurt
1 tsp vanilla essence
85 g/3 oz fresh blueberries

Fruity Muffins

very easy

makes 10

prep: 15 minutes +
cooling

25–30 minutes cooking

280 g/10 oz self-raising
wholemeal flour
2 tsp baking powder
2 tbsp brown sugar
85 g/3 oz no-soak dried apricots,
finely chopped
1 banana, mashed with
1 tbsp orange juice
1 tsp finely grated
orange rind
300 ml/10 fl oz skimmed milk
1 egg, beaten
3 tbsp sunflower or peanut oil
2 tbsp rolled oats
fruit spread, honey or maple syrup,
to serve

Preheat the oven to 200°C/400°F/Gas Mark 6. Line 10 cups of a 12-cup muffin tin with muffin paper cases.

Sift the flour and baking powder into a mixing bowl, adding any husks that remain in the sieve. Stir in the sugar and chopped apricots.

Make a well in the centre and add the mashed banana, orange rind, milk, egg and oil. Mix together well to form a thick mixture and divide the mixture evenly between the muffin cases.

Sprinkle with a few rolled oats and bake in the preheated oven for 25–30 minutes until well risen and firm to the touch or until a cocktail stick inserted into the centre comes out clean.

Remove the muffins from the oven and place them on a wire rack to cool slightly. Serve the muffins while still warm with a little fruit spread, honey or maple syrup.

Cranberry Muffins

Preheat the oven to 200°C/400°F/Gas Mark 6. Lightly grease 18 cups in 2 x 12-cup muffin tins.

Sift the flour, baking powder and salt into a mixing bowl. Stir in the caster sugar.

In a separate bowl, mix the butter, eggs and milk together, then pour into the bowl of dry ingredients. Mix lightly together until the ingredients are evenly combined. Finally, stir in the fresh cranberries.

Divide the mixture between the prepared muffin tins. Sprinkle the grated Parmesan cheese over the top of each muffin. Bake in the preheated oven for about 20 minutes, or until the muffins are well risen and a golden brown colour.

Remove the muffins from the oven and leave to cool in the tins, then carefully transfer to a wire rack and leave to cool completely before serving.

very easy

makes 18

prep : 15 minutes + cooling

20 minutes cooking

butter, for greasing
225 g/8 oz plain flour
2 tsp baking powder
$^1/_2$ tsp salt
50 g/1$^3/_4$ oz caster sugar
4 tbsp butter, melted
2 eggs, beaten
200 ml/7 fl oz milk
100 g/3$^1/_2$ oz fresh cranberries
35 g/1$^1/_4$ oz Parmesan cheese, freshly grated

Scones

easy

makes 16

prep: 20 minutes

10–12 minutes cooking

450 g/1 lb plain flour
$^1/_2$ tsp salt
2 tsp baking powder
55 g/2 oz butter
2 tbsp caster sugar
250 ml/9 fl oz milk
3 tbsp milk, for glazing
strawberry jam and clotted cream, to serve

Preheat the oven to 220°C/425°F/Gas Mark 7.

Sift the flour, salt and baking powder into a bowl. Rub in the butter until the mixture resembles breadcrumbs. Stir in the sugar.

Make a well in the centre and pour in the milk. Stir in using a round-bladed knife and make a soft dough.

Turn the mixture onto a floured surface and lightly flatten the dough until it is of an even thickness, about 1 cm/$^1/_2$ inch. Don't be heavy-handed: scones need a light touch.

Use a 6-cm/2$^1/_2$-inch pastry cutter to cut out the scones and place on the baking tray.

Glaze with a little milk and bake in the preheated oven for 10–12 minutes, until golden and well risen.

Cool on a wire rack and serve freshly baked with strawberry jam and clotted cream.

Oaty Pecan Cookies

Preheat the oven to 180°C/350°F/Gas Mark 4, and grease 2 baking sheets. Place the butter and sugar in a bowl and beat until light and fluffy. Gradually beat in the egg, then stir in the nuts.

Sift the flour and baking powder into the mixture and add the oats. Stir together until well combined. Drop dessertspoonfuls of the mixture onto the prepared baking sheets, spaced well apart to allow for spreading.

Bake in the preheated oven for 15 minutes, or until pale golden. Leave to cool on the baking sheets for 2 minutes, then transfer to wire racks to cool completely.

very easy

makes 15

prep: 10 minutes +
20 minutes cooling

15 minutes cooking

115 g/4 oz butter, softened, plus extra for greasing
85 g/3 oz light muscovado sugar
1 egg, beaten
55 g/2 oz pecan nuts, chopped
85 g/3 oz plain flour
$^1/_2$ tsp baking powder
55 g/2 oz rolled oats

Rock Drops

very easy

makes 8

prep: 15 minutes + cooling

15-20 minutes cooking

100 g/3¹/₂ oz butter, diced, plus
extra for greasing
200 g/7 oz plain flour
2 tsp baking powder
75 g/2³/₄ oz demerara sugar
100 g/3¹/₂ oz sultanas
25 g/1 oz glacé cherries,
finely chopped
1 egg, beaten
2 tbsp milk

Preheat the oven to 200°C/400°F/Gas Mark 6. Lightly grease a baking tray with a little butter.

Sift the flour and baking powder into a mixing bowl. Rub in the butter with your fingertips until the mixture resembles breadcrumbs. Stir in the sugar, sultanas and chopped glacé cherries. Add the beaten egg and milk to the mixture and bring together to form a soft dough.

Spoon 8 mounds of the mixture onto the prepared baking tray, spaced well apart to allow room to expand during cooking.

Bake in the preheated oven for 15–20 minutes, until firm to the touch. Remove the rock drops from the baking tray. Serve piping hot from the oven, or transfer to a wire rack and leave to cool before serving.

Orange & Walnut Cakes

easy

makes 18

prep: 20 minutes +
cooling

20 minutes cooking

400 g/14 oz self-raising flour
$^1/_2$ tsp bicarbonate of soda
$^1/_2$ tsp ground cinnamon
$^1/_4$ tsp ground cloves
pinch of grated nutmeg
pinch of salt
300 ml/10 fl oz olive oil
75 g/2$^3/_4$ oz caster sugar
finely grated rind and juice
of 1 large orange

TOPPING

25 g/1 oz walnut pieces,
finely chopped
$^1/_2$ tsp ground cinnamon

SYRUP

175 g/6 oz Greek honey
125 ml/4 fl oz water
juice of 1 small lemon
juice of 1 small orange or 1 tbsp
orange flower water

Preheat the oven to 180°C/350°F/Gas Mark 4. Sift together the flour, bicarbonate of soda, cinnamon, cloves, nutmeg and salt.

Put the oil and sugar in a bowl and beat together. Add the orange rind and juice then gradually beat in the flour mixture. Turn the mixture onto a lightly floured surface and knead for 2–3 minutes, until smooth.

Take small, egg-sized pieces of dough and shape into ovals. Place on baking trays, allowing room for spreading and, with the back of a fork, press the top of each twice to make a criss-cross design.

Bake the cakes in the preheated oven for about 20 minutes, until lightly browned. Transfer to a wire rack and leave to cool.

Meanwhile, make the topping by mixing together the walnuts and cinnamon. To make the syrup, put the honey and water in a saucepan, bring to the boil then simmer for 5 minutes. Remove from the heat and add the lemon juice and orange juice or orange flower water.

When the cakes have almost cooled, using a slotted spoon, submerge each cake in the hot syrup and leave for about 1 minute. Place on a tray and top each with the walnut mixture. Leave until cold before serving.

Butter Cookies

easy

makes 36

prep: 15 minutes + cooling

15 minutes cooking

175 g/6 oz butter
140 g/5 oz caster sugar
1 egg
280 g/10 oz self-raising flour, plus extra for dusting
finely grated rind of 1 lemon
20 g/³/₄ oz flaked almonds (optional)

Preheat the oven to 180°C/350°F/Gas Mark 4. Put the butter and sugar in a bowl and whisk together until light and fluffy. Whisk in the egg then fold in the flour and lemon rind.

Turn out the dough onto a lightly floured surface and knead gently until smooth. Form the mixture into rolls the thickness of a finger then cut into 10-cm/4-inch lengths. Shape each roll into an S shape and place on baking trays, allowing room for spreading. If liked, stud with a few flaked almonds.

Bake the cookies in the preheated oven for about 15 minutes, until lightly browned. Cool on a wire rack. Store the cookies in an airtight tin.

Peanut Butter Cookies

Preheat the oven to 190°C/375°F/Gas Mark 5. Lightly grease 2 baking trays with a little butter.

Beat the butter and peanut butter together in a large mixing bowl. Gradually add the granulated sugar and beat well. Add the beaten egg, a little at a time, beating well after each addition until thoroughly blended.

Sift the flour, baking powder and salt into the creamed peanut butter mixture.

Add the chopped peanuts and bring the mixture together with your fingers to form a soft dough. Wrap in clingfilm and chill in the refrigerator for about 30 minutes.

Form the dough into 20 balls and place them on the prepared baking trays, spaced well apart to allow room to expand during cooking. Flatten them slightly with your hand.

Bake in the preheated oven for 15 minutes, until golden brown. Transfer the biscuits to a wire rack and leave to cool before serving.

easy

makes 20

prep: 15 minutes + cooling/chilling

15 minutes cooking

125 g/4^1/$_2$ oz butter, softened, plus extra for greasing
150 g/5^1/$_2$ oz chunky peanut butter
225 g/8 oz granulated sugar
1 egg, lightly beaten
150 g/5^1/$_2$ oz plain flour
^{1}/$_2$ tsp baking powder
pinch of salt
75 g/2^3/$_4$ oz peanuts, chopped

INDEX